Rad Sports
Mountain Biking
Techniques and Tricks

Aaron Rosenberg

Published in 2003 by The Rosen Publishing Group, Inc.
29 East 21st Street, New York, NY 10010

Copyright © 2003 by The Rosen Publishing Group, Inc.

First Edition

All rights reserved. No part of this book may be reproduced in any form without permission in writing from the publisher, except by a reviewer.

Library of Congress Cataloging-in-Publication Data

Rosenberg, Aaron.
Mountain Biking: Techniques and Tricks / by Aaron Rosenberg.— 1st ed.
   p. cm. — (Rad sports)
Summary: Discusses the history of the sport of mountain biking, the necessary equipment, cross country and downhill racing, and the specific techniques involved.
Includes bibliographical references and index.
ISBN 978-1-4358-9069-5
1. All terrain cycling—Juvenile literature. [1. All terrain cycling.] I. Title. II. Series.
GV1056 .R67 2003
796.6'3—dc21

2002012245

Manufactured in the United States of America

CONTENTS

	Introduction	5
Chapter 1	Fat-Tire Fever	6
Chapter 2	Riding Skills for Beginners	12
Chapter 3	Trail Techniques and Tricks	17
Chapter 4	The Right Bike for You	33
	Glossary	42
	For More Information	43
	For Further Reading	45
	Bibliography	46
	Index	47

Introduction

Remember when biking meant riding down the street to the store, or riding in circles around the playground? Well, those days are long gone!

Mountain biking takes the bicycle off roads and streets and into the countryside, onto rough terrain that requires skill to negotiate. When bicyclists first took to off-road trails, they wanted to get away from crowded and dangerous streets. What they found was a natural landscape that tested their riding skills, their endurance, and the bicycle itself. And as soon as there were two or more people on a trail, competition became part of the riding experience. This included competition between the rider and the terrain. Off-road riders knew they had found something special.

Mountain biking is an exciting sport and one that's become more and more popular over the last twenty years. It's even in the Olympics! Mountain biking has it all—speed, excitement, scenery, and freedom. It's you against the earth, struggling over every rock and root, and the feel of conquering that path is exhilarating.

Chapter 1

Fat-Tire Fever

Mountain biking is really a new sport that began in the 1970s. The idea of riding a bicycle on rough ground, however, dates back as far as the turn of the twentieth century. That was when the Buffalo Soldiers (an all-black army group training in the American West) rebuilt bicycles so they could carry gear over rough ground from Montana to Yellowstone National Park in Wyoming, and back. Their experiment was to see whether the bikes could be used for military purposes.

In the 1950s, bicyclists in Paris, France, started the Velo Cross Club Parisien (VCCP). The VCCP had about twenty bicyclists, all from the outskirts of Paris, and the club members modified their bikes for off-road use. At about the same time in the United States, a man named John Finley Scott built what he called a Woodsie Bike. The Woodsie had a Schwinn-made frame but used balloon tires, flat handlebars, derailleur (gear-changer device) gears, and cantilever (scissor-shaped) brakes. Scott was probably the first mountain-biking enthusiast.

Then, in the early 1970s, the sport of mountain biking began with the "klunkers." The group got its name from their bikes, which were old one-speed "klunkers," heavier bikes than the modern road racers, but more solid and capable of taking a beating on rough ground. Gary Fisher and Charles Kelly were among the first klunkers, bikers from San Francisco who grew sick of the city and moved to quieter Marin County, California. That's where they met a man named Joe Breeze and his friend Tom Ritchey. Breeze and Ritchey were also bikers, but they liked to bike off road instead of on black-top surfaces. Fisher and Kelly began biking with them and discovered the joys of biking on rough terrain.

Fisher and Kelly organized races in the area and began improving the bikes they rode. They wanted to build bicycles that were sturdier, had better brakes, and had tires with traction. The klunkers had only a frame, tires, a seat, handlebars, pedals, and a chain. They called their new bikes "cyclocross" bikes, because they were more versatile than standard models.

The First Bicycles

Everything has to start someplace, and it's interesting to see where and when some of the biking innovations first began. In 1816, the German baron Karl von Drais built a "draisine." This

Bicycles from different eras appear in this picture taken in 1950. The high-wheeled bicycle *(left)* was first built in England in the 1870s. An early version of a road bicycle *(right)* from the 1950s has the curled handlebars that are popular today.

Biking Conduct

Mountain biking is a sport, which means it has rules. And not all of them are for racing. The most important rules are simply about conduct—how to handle yourself and your bike around others in order to show respect and get along properly. Here are the basics:

1. Learn proper riding techniques.

2. Ride only on designated trails, and don't cause any damage. Do not ride when it's wet or muddy.

3. Before starting a ride, make sure your bike is in good working condition. Check to see that you have spare parts, adequate food, water, clothing, and a small first-aid kit.

4. Yield to others—slow down or stop when approaching someone on the trail.

5. Let others know you're there.

6. Be polite and don't cause trouble.

7. Watch for wildlife and livestock and give them plenty of room.

8. Bike with a buddy.

Fat-Tire Fever

> 9. When heading out, leave word with someone about your route and destination, and when you'll be back.
>
> 10. Always help protect the environment. Remember: garbage in, garbage out!
>
> 11. On the highway, a biker has the same rights and duties as someone driving a car. Know the laws and obey them.

bike had two wheels, but no chain or pedals. The rider had to propel himself or herself by foot, as if on a sort of high-chair scooter. The bike was made of wood and only a handful of wealthy people owned one to use as an alternative to strolling through gardens.

By 1887, bicycles had pedals and chains. Riders used mostly solid tires that had no air. Then, in that same year, Irish veterinary surgeon John B. Dunlop fitted a piece of rubber hose inside his son's bicycle tire. This was the first pneumatic (air-filled) tire. Later, bicycle tires with a diameter of two inches first appeared in the early 1930s in Germany and America. They were called balloon tires.

Russ Mahon, of Cupertino, California, was probably the first person to ride a "fat bike" off road with a derailleur, back in 1973. This was also the first fat-tire bike with both a derailleur and good brakes. Gary Fisher copied the idea a year or two later, between 1974 and 1975.

The modern mountain bike has state-of-the-art parts that help riders pedal easier, climb faster, absorb bumps, and stop quickly.

Joe Breeze gets credit for the first fat-tire bike with an off-road frame and all new parts. He built ten Breezer #1s in Marin County in 1977. Two years later, Tom Ritchey of Redwood City, California, started building fat-tire frames. Ritchey's frames were sold by Fisher and Kelly through their new company, MountainBikes (which later became the Gary Fisher Bicycle Company). They were the first fat-tire bikes to be widely available. MountainBikes was also the first company to sell only mountain bikes.

In 1982, the Specialized Stumpjumper and the Univega Alpina Pro were sold in bicycle stores. These were the first mountain bikes to be both widely available and priced under a thousand dollars.

Competition

Racing against others is exciting, even more so than solo mountain biking. Don't compete until you're ready, however.

The National Off-Road Bicycle Association (NORBA) sponsors competitions throughout the United States. The contact info for NORBA is listed in the For More Information section at the back of this book.

You need to be physically fit in order to compete at any level. This takes practice, training, and the proper diet. Both amateurs and professionals maintain a training program year-round so they are ready to compete. Exercise off the bike is as important as training on the bike. Check out one of the books listed in the For Further Reading section at the back of this book to find a sample training and diet program.

Competition Disciplines:

Cross-Country and Downhill

Cross-country mountain biking is all about distance and endurance. Races can run several hours, and usually it's less about speed than about pacing, strategy, and stamina. Cross-country tours are even more grueling, because you might be on the bike for days at a time. Still, it's exhilarating to cover that kind of distance, and the races test your mind as much as your body.

Downhill is the more popular of the two mountain biking disciplines. Downhill competition is all about speed, with courses ranging from under a minute to about ten minutes, and involves twists, turns, and a lot of obstacles. Downhill biking is definitely not for the timid, and it has far more chances for injury than cross-country biking. Still, this is what got a lot of people into the sport in the first place—the sense of freedom and danger as you careen down a mountain, weaving around trees and rocks.

Chapter 2

Riding Skills for Beginners

Mountain biking is more complicated than just getting on your bike and riding into the woods. But that's part of what makes it fun—going downhill, making quick turns, dodging roots and fallen trees, and climbing hills. Mountain biking's popularity has grown from this diversity of sport.

Braking

Learning to use your brakes properly is essential for safe biking. When you're mountain biking, you will need to brake quickly to avoid obstacles or sudden drops. The lever on the right controls your back brake, and the left lever controls the front brake. The front brake is much stronger than the back brake because your weight shifts forward as you brake. More weight

Riding Skills for Beginners

riding on your front wheel gives it more traction. This increased traction gives the front brake more power. Practice gaining speed and then stopping so you understand the physics of braking.

1. At low speeds, you want to squeeze both levers at once, but put a little more pressure on the back tire (the right lever).
2. At high speeds, you should raise your butt off the saddle and shift back. Now your body is better balanced for high-speed or downhill braking. In this position, you can apply the front brake more firmly and stop more quickly.

In some cases, your back tire may skid. When that happens, feather the front brake (pump the brake using light pressure). Feather the front brake lightly enough so that the bike doesn't jerk.

Be careful about braking in the rain. Anticipate when you need to slow down (nearing a downhill trail section or coming into technical turns) and pump both the front and back brakes to brush away the water from the rim. Now you have more stopping power when you really need it.

Mountain Biking: Techniques and Tricks

Shifting Gears

Gears determine how much tension is in the bike chain. A higher gear gives you more speed, while a lower gear gives you more climbing power. You'll use every gear on almost every ride when you ride a mountain bike.

Both a trigger shift (top) and a grip shift (bottom) let you shift gears without taking your hands off the handlebar grips.

There are two types of gear shifters available for mountain bikes: the trigger shifter and the grip shifter. Both work smoothly to give you quick gear-changing action. You'll need it when you begin riding rougher terrain. Neither is better than the other, just different. Test which you like before you buy your bike.

Learning which gear you should be in will help you bike better. Practice feeling the gears. As you shift, you can feel the amount of tension in the chain.

The gear you want to be in depends on the terrain and your normal strength. What you want most is to be able to pedal without much strain so you don't tire yourself out to the point where you need to stop.

Never force the gears. It damages the drive train and the front and rear derailleurs. When you shift, release pressure on your pedal stroke, make the shift, and then continue on. That way the shift is smoother. Shift one gear at a time, unless you need to shift suddenly. Try to anticipate your surroundings; if you know the hill is about to rise, get ready to shift to a different gear.

Riding Skills for Beginners

Trackstand

A trackstand is when you come to a complete stop and stay balanced in one place without your feet touching the ground. Being able to trackstand lets you stop and rest for a few seconds without having to get off your bike. Once you can balance while standing, try doing this seated as well.

1. Come to a complete stop with your pedals parallel to the ground and your "good foot" (your dominant foot) forward. Turn your handlebars about thirty degrees in the opposite direction from your good foot (if you're right-foot dominant, turn your handlebars to the left). You can also rest your opposite leg against the frame

2. To stay balanced, turn your front wheel an inch or more in either direction until you feel the bike will fall. Keep shifting your weight and the wheel smoothly to stay balanced.

Mountain Biking: Techniques and Tricks

Spinning

There's a lot more to pedaling than just pushing down on the lead pedals each rotation. Proper pedaling, or spinning, requires pedaling at high revolutions per minute (RPM)—also known as high cadence with low resistance. Spinning lets you ride faster and farther without using as much effort or energy.

1. Maintain pedaling strokes of 60 to 90 RPMs. Don't worry about pushing hard on the downstroke—the idea is to use your leg force in a circular motion. This means you are pedaling on both the downstroke and the upstroke.

2. Spinning lets you add power throughout the entire stroke, instead of just on the downstroke. It takes some practice to get used to this, but after a while you'll feel the difference.

3. To check your cadence, count the number of times one leg comes up to the top of its pedal stroke in thirty seconds, then double that number. The result is your RPM.

Chapter 3

Trail Techniques and Tricks

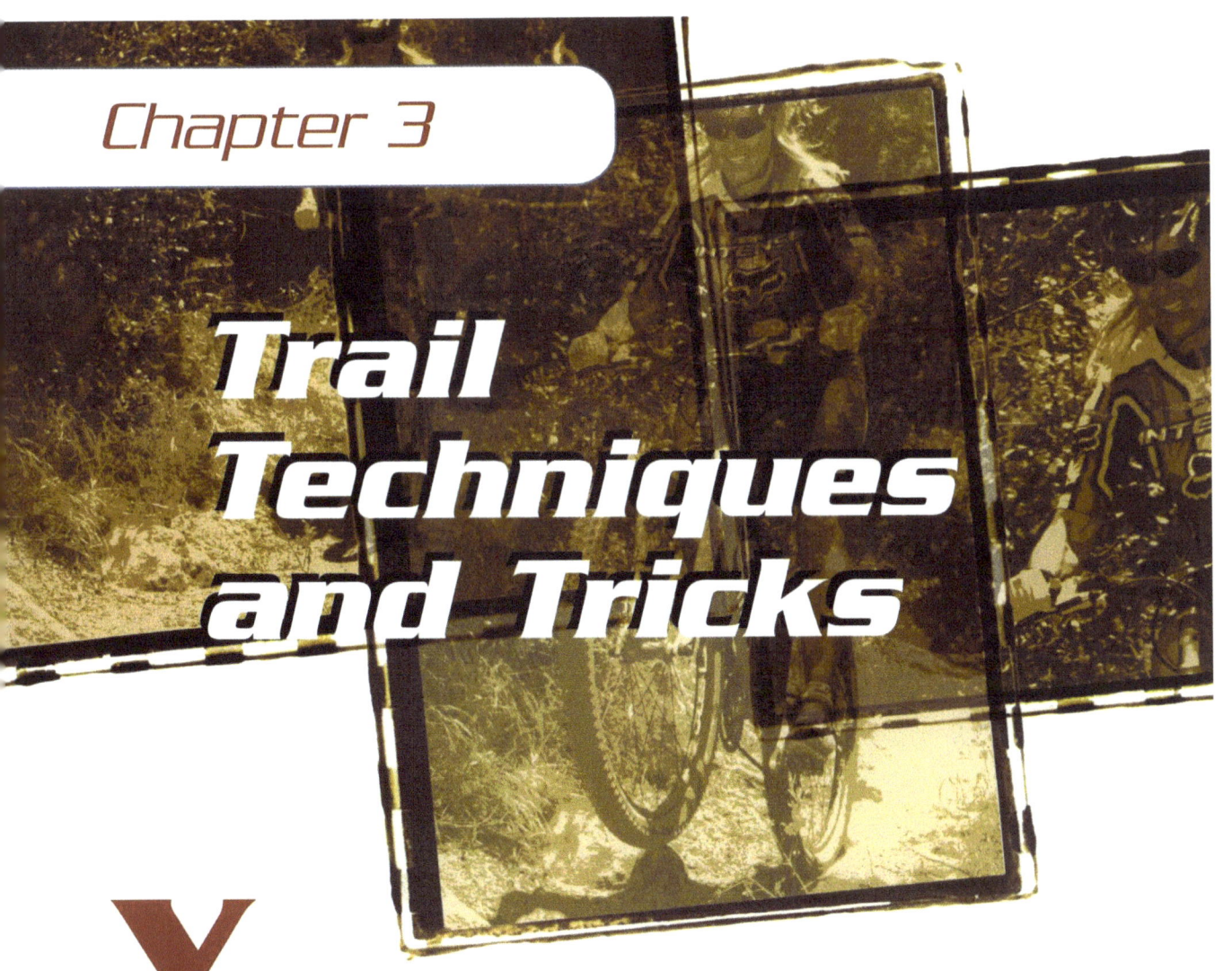

You can ride a mountain bike well, or you can ride it poorly. There really is no third way. The difference is technique. Proper riding techniques—for climbing, descending, technical turning, and getting over obstacles—give you the ability to ride smoothly and quickly for a long time, and lessen the chance for a crash or injury. The following techniques are tried-and-true and will get you started on good riding habits.

Climbing Hills: Seated and Standing

You have two options when you climb: You can stay seated or you can stand. Think about the terrain you're going to climb, the incline, and the length of the climb. Sitting is better for long distances and loose terrain, while standing works better for short, steep sections.

Mountain Biking: Techniques and Tricks

The Seated Climb

1. Shift to a lower gear and slide forward onto the narrow section of the saddle (seat). This moves your weight over the bottom bracket and makes your pedaling more efficient.

2. Keep your head low and close to your handlebars to keep the front wheel from bouncing up.

Don't pull up on the handlebars. Pull backward and down instead. This pushes the rear wheel into the ground, where it won't easily slip. Try to stay relaxed and loose during the climb; tensing up wastes energy.

The Standing Climb

When you come to a steep but short uphill section, a standing climb will give you the best position for balance and power.

1. First, shift down to a climbing gear (between 1 and 5 will do). Stay low and keep your weight even—you want enough weight over the rear wheel to keep from slipping, and enough weight over the front to keep it from lifting.

2. Move your hands out to the bar ends for better leverage, and pedal steadily. Concentrate on breathing evenly to keep from getting winded too quickly before you reach the top of the uphill section.

3. When you get to the top and level off, shift up, sit down, and pick up your speed.

Mountain Biking: Techniques and Tricks

Technical Climbs

Technical climbs take more concentration and effort because you've got to maintain momentum and get around obstacles at the same time.

1. As you come to the hill, look for the smoothest line possible.

2. Spot obstacles beforehand so you can prepare; if there are tree roots or rocks, you may need to lift your front wheel to get over them.

3. Take the line you've sighted and turn the front wheel as you move up and around the obstacles.

Trail Techniques and Tricks

Stay seated as long as possible, even if you have to use the lowest gear. Standing will only make it harder to get good traction on the obstacles. If you do stand, stay low and keep your weight over the rear wheel. When you do hit an obstacle, keep pedaling to maintain your momentum. Once you're past the obstacle, settle back down on the seat and keep pedaling.

Descending

OK, you got up the hill. As hills go, though, what you bike up must also be biked down. Descending techniques require good handling and braking skills. It's best to set up your body position before you come to any downhill section.

1. First, level your pedals so they're parallel to the ground. Scan the trail ahead of you for any obstacles or trouble spots. Don't focus on trouble spots, though—you should keep your eyes on the line you want to run, not the obstacles you're hoping to avoid.

2. Keep your weight back and off the saddle. The steeper the trail, the farther back and closer to the rear wheel your butt should be. This will keep you from going endo (over the handlebars).

Mountain Biking: Techniques and Tricks

3. Descending (continued)

3. Use enough front brake to keep your speed under control, but not too much or you could halt or skid. Use the rear brake only if you start to slide or skid, and only enough to regain control.

Keep your body flexible to absorb shocks. Your hands should grip the bars firmly, but not tight enough that the front wheel jerks if it hits rocks or roots. Remember that braking is crucial to successful descents.

Technical Descents

Technical descents require careful braking, steering, and weight transfer. Again, set up your body position before rolling into any descent.

1. Map out the line as you roll into the descent. Choose a line that has the least number of rocks, roots, or ruts to negotiate. You may need to ride over a tough spot or two in order to get a smoother line beyond that point.

2. Zigzag around obstacles rather than bulling right into them; it's all about control, and you've got better control if you aren't bouncing over a large root.

3. Keep your knees bent a little to absorb shocks, and pedal kick (see page 28) around smaller obstacles. You should also maintain a moderate speed: too slow and you may stall, too fast and you could lose control.

Cornering

Always slow down with both brakes before entering a turn, then accelerate during the turn and as you come out of it.

1. Enter the turn wide and drift toward the inside edge—this lets you corner safely at higher speeds.

Mountain Biking: Techniques and Tricks

2. Cornering (continued)

2. Lean your upper body toward the inside of the turn, and point your inside leg and knee in that direction, with your weight on the outside pedal. This gives you more traction and stability. Look toward the inside of the turn as well.

3. Exit the turn wide to maintain balance and speed.

Cornering on loose terrain is risky because your front wheel could skid. To avoid this, lean your weight forward to give the front wheel more grip. If you feel the rear wheel starting to skid, don't lean back—just release the rear brake. In really loose terrain, like deep sand, lean your weight in the direction of the turn and bend your knees to the side to keep the bike upright. Let the bike run through sand; oversteering will dump you off your bike.

Trail Techniques and Tricks

Downhill Switchbacks

A downhill switchback is a turn so tight that you literally end up going in the opposite direction as you come out of the turn.

1. As with a normal corner, slow down as you enter the switchback and enter wide.

2. Drift toward the inside edge as you come through the middle of the switchback. (You may have to put your inside foot down to help pivot the bike.) Move your weight back and onto the outside pedal. Then lean your body far into the corner.

3. As you roll out of the switchback, release the brakes and continue down the hill.

Mountain Biking: Techniques and Tricks

Obstacles: Roots, Rocks, and Ruts

Obstacles are a fact of mountain biking—and part of the fun! Properly negotiating roots, rocks, and ruts is a must to get the most from your rides.

Riding Over Rocks and Roots

1. In order to clear small rocks and roots, yank up on your handlebars and give a moderately forceful pedal kick (described on page 28). This should compress your front wheel and pop it up onto or over the obstacle.

2. Once up or over the obstacle, level out your pedals and transfer your weight forward so the rear wheel can roll up and over. This lets you maintain your momentum, whereas running into roots and rocks slows you down.

Ruts need to be handled differently. Ruts running across the trail can be ridden over easily—just keep your hands loose and your body flexible to take the jarring bumps. Ruts running at an angle to or parallel with the trail are more tricky. If handled incorrectly, a rut can grab either wheel and send you flying into the brush or, worse, a tree. Try to avoid riding in the rut. If that's not possible, try the following technique.

Trail Techniques and Tricks

Riding Through Ruts

1. Slow down and let your wheels go into the rut.

2. Ride the line that the rut takes you. Don't try to turn against it, but stand low with your knees bent and slowly steer along with it. Keep your body weight back to maintain control of the bike.

3. When the rut ends, pick a new, better line down the trail.

Mountain Biking: Techniques and Tricks

Pedal Kick

The pedal kick is extremely helpful when trying to get over obstacles. It pops your front wheel up instead of running it into an obstacle head-on.

1. To pedal kick, level your pedals so they're parallel to the ground.

2. Backstroke your stronger leg to raise the pedal at a forty-five degree angle. As your front wheel reaches the root, drive that leg forward about a quarter-turn.

3. A quick pedal kick will launch your front wheel up, either over or on top of the obstacle. (You can practice your pedal kick on a sidewalk curb before heading to the mountains. Just ride straight toward the curb, then pedal kick your front wheel up onto it.)

Trail Techniques and Tricks

The Bunny Hop

Bunny hopping is used to jump your bike onto or over an obstacle. The name comes from how a rabbit hops: The front legs rise first, with the hind legs following. A good bunny hop can get you over logs, rocks, mud, and water without forcing you to get off your bike to walk it around the obstacle.

1. Slow down as you come to the obstacle, then come to a complete stop in front of the obstacle, with both brakes engaged and your good foot forward.

2. Shift your weight back and pull the front of the bike off the ground.

3. Then shift your weight forward and pull your hips up and forward. This should bring the back tire up. Use your legs to help pull it off the ground.

Mountain Biking: Techniques and Tricks

Don't try bunny hopping in motion until you've mastered it in a static position. To bunny hop in motion, do the same as above but without the brakes. Start out by riding along slowly and pulling a small hop. You'll need to pull your front end up a bit higher than you did while you were static, but if you've done it right you should "hop" over the obstacle.

The Hop

You can use a hop to jump small logs, mud, or puddles. The hop is executed while moving. Practice hops without obstacles blocking your path until you're comfortable with the technique. Once you master the hop, you can use it going slow or fast.

1. Ride along at a moderate speed and level your pedals with your good foot forward. Keep your body low, with your knees and arms bent.

2. Bring your weight up, then drop it down to compress the front shocks. As the shocks come up, lift your body with it and pull yourself and the bike into the air.

Trail Techniques and Tricks

3. As you come down past the obstacle, land with your pedals level and knees bent to absorb the shock.

It takes practice to feel the momentum for when you crunch down and lift up. A good hop will bring your bike more than a foot off the ground. When you have the timing down, you can start hopping over logs.

The Drop-Off

Some obstacles are large in area and can bring you more than a knee's length off the ground. You'll go over these large obstacles frequently on some trails, so it's best to learn a proven technique to drop off them and keep on riding.

1. Slowly pedal toward the edge of the obstacle. As you get to the edge, pull a small wheelie or pedal kick (while sitting) and pedal off the obstacle.

Mountain Biking: Techniques and Tricks

② The Drop-Off (continued) ③

2. As your bike falls, stand up. This brings the front end down a little.

3. When you land, the rear wheel should hit first, then the front. Bend your knees to absorb the shock. (Be careful not to pull the wheelie too high, or you'll land on your back instead of on both wheels.)

To drop off while moving, accelerate to a decent speed so your momentum can carry the bike off the drop. Then lean back a bit and try to touch down with the rear wheel just before the front one, so that you don't sail over the handlebars.

You will probably use each technique described on every ride. Trails are unpredictable because nature and geology are always changing them. A fallen tree here, a newly formed rut there, and you will find the skills you've learned here are put to good use. The best thing thing you can do for yourself as a mountain bike rider is to practice these techniques on the trails you ride most often. This way you will be ready to keep yourself on the bike and able to stay out of trouble on trails with which you are most familiar riding.

Chapter 4

The Right Bike for You

Mountain bikes and the gears that riders use for off-road cycling are specially made for rough use. Understanding the needs of the sport and your needs as a rider will help you determine which bike is best for you. Finding the right mountain bike is the best way to get the most for your money, time, and effort.

Buying a Mountain Bike

Before you buy a bike, think about what you want to do with it. If you're only going to go off road on rough terrain, you need a true mountain bike. But if you want to do both paved-surface and off-road riding, you should look at a hybrid bicycle (modified using the latest hi-tech equipment) instead.

Mountain Biking: Techniques and Tricks

Then think about how much you want to spend. Bikes can cost from $300 to more than $3,000. More expensive bikes tend to be made from lighter, stronger materials such as carbon fiber compounds. They will likely have disc brake systems, high-performance shock absorbers, and state-of-the-art gear systems. When you're starting out, you should stick with a less expensive bike that has all the basics—V-brakes, front shocks, and Shimano gears—without worrying about the extras just yet.

Always test-ride a bike before you buy it. You need to make sure you buy a bike that fits your body size and that works as comfortably for you as possible. This means checking how your grip feels on the handlebars, how your feet feel on the pedals, and that gear shifting is comfortable for your hands (and does not distract you from keeping your eyes on the trail!). You should be able to stand on the ground and straddle the frame comfortably—that's the frame, not the seat. There should be at least an inch between your crotch and the top bar.

Also, make sure the bike comes with a warranty. If any problems or breakdowns happen in the first year, you should have the ability to take it in for repair free of charge. And, if at all possible, shop near where you live—that way, when the bike needs service, you can take it back to the shop where you bought it.

Bicycle Adjustments

Every bicycle needs to be adjusted to fit your body size properly. Things such as saddle height, brake and pedal clip tension, and handlebar height affect how comfortable—and safe—your ride will be. If you purchase a bike from a shop, the experts there should offer to adjust the bike for you. Let them help you, since they know how best to set up your bike for your particular body size. This will also give you the opportunity to see how it's done so that you can do it yourself later on.

Once you start riding, give yourself some time to get used to the bike. Then, if you still don't feel completely comfortable, you can either take it back for a refit or tinker with it yourself. Ultimately, you should be as comfortable on it as possible, so you're the final judge of what works and what doesn't.

Pedals

Most people think that the pedal should be placed under the arch of the foot. This position is actually not efficient and often very uncomfortable. The ball of your foot should be directly over the spindle, so that the pedals crank smoothly and naturally. If you're using clipless (sometimes called clip-in) pedals, just shift the cleat to the right place for your foot. If you've got toe clips, make sure the clip is the right length to guide your foot into the proper position. There should be a small gap between the front of the clip and the toe of your shoe.

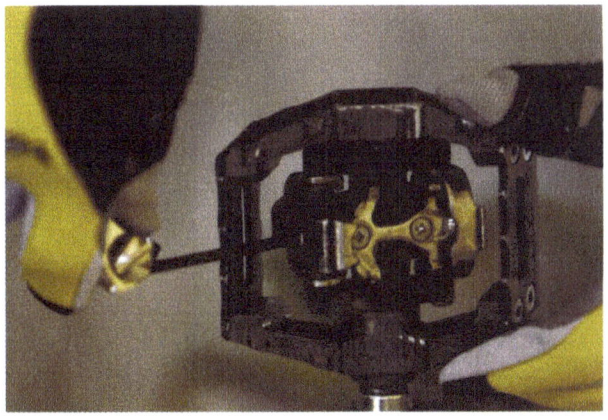

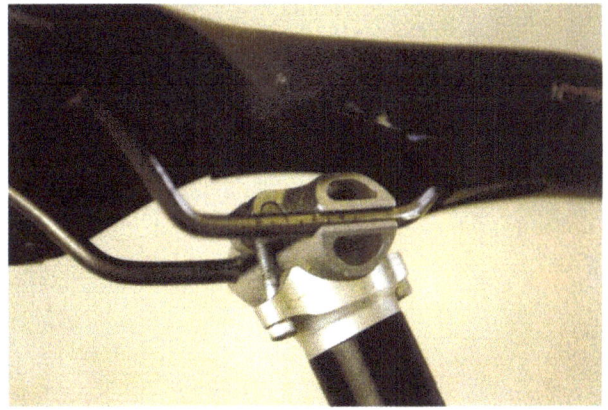

Saddle

With the saddle, you need to look at two different aspects: height and angle. The height of the saddle affects

Adjusting pedals (top) and the saddle (bottom) properly helps you avoid injury and body fatigue by making the bike fit better to your size and weight.

the motion of your legs during each pedal stroke. Once your feet are set you need to make sure you've got the height right. At the bottom of each stroke, your knee should be almost straight (but bent slightly), and at the top it should be bent sharply. You want the seat high, to reduce knee stress on the downstroke, but not so high that the knee hyperextends on the downstroke. This will cut your power and potentially harm the front of your knee.

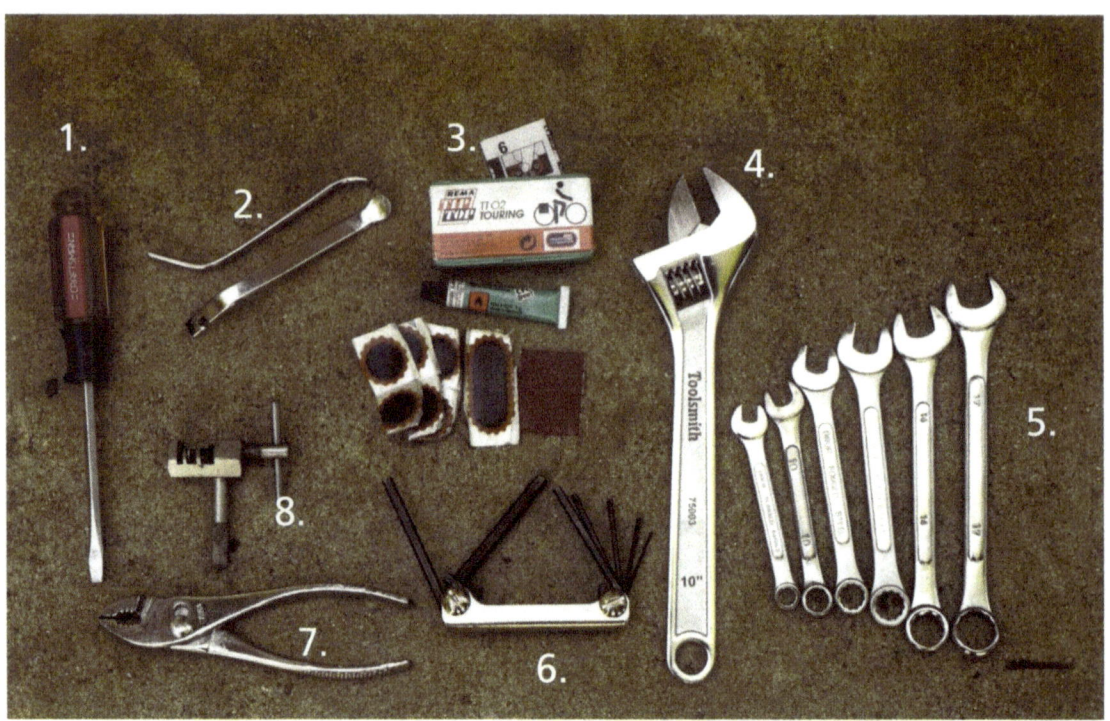

You should get a set of basic tools so that you can maintain your bike properly. Bike shops may have them in preassembled tool kits, but if not you can find them individually at hardware stores and bike shops:
1. small slothead (standard) screwdriver **2.** tire levers **3.** tube patch kit **4.** adjustable wrench **5.** open-end metric wrenches, in sizes 17, 16, 15, 14, 10, 9, and 8 mm **6.** Allen wrenches, in sizes 6, 5, and 4 mm **7.** pair of standard pliers **8.** chain rivet tool

Fortunately, mountain bike seats are easy to adjust. Many have a quick-release lever to make adjustment even easier. Just watch the seat post when you're adjusting it. There is a safe-height line inscribed there, and you can't pull the seat above that. If you do need to go higher, buy a longer seat post.

Once you've got the saddle at the right height, you need to adjust its tilt and forward/rear position. This adjustment also affects your knees and determines how powerfully you can pedal. As you sit on the bike with the pedal in its level forward position, there should be a straight line down from the bone just below your kneecap, through the ball of your foot, and finally through the spindle of the pedal. If you're adjusting the seat yourself, have a friend stand nearby and eyeball the position as you sit. You can adjust the

The Right Bike for You

saddle by loosening the bolt underneath. Don't take the nut or bolt off if you can avoid it, as they can be tricky to put back on.

For saddle tilt, you want your weight distributed evenly. If it's tilted too far forward, you're leaning on your hands, but if it's too far back, the weight is on your groin. Men should start with the saddle level or tilted slightly upward in front. Women may want it tilted slightly downward, especially if using a unisex saddle. You can adjust the tilt while fixing the position; the same clamp controls both. Most saddles have notches for tilt, so you'll need to adjust it by full notches until you find the most comfortable position.

Handlebars

Handlebars also have two adjustments: height and tilt. Adjusting handlebar height is all about making yourself comfortable. A higher handlebar stops you from bending your lower back too far and keeps the weight off your hands.

Start with the handlebars an inch lower than the top of the saddle. The higher the bar, the more wind resistance you'll get, but the more comfortable you'll be. Handlebar stems have safe-height lines, the same way saddle posts do. When you adjust the stem, make sure you don't go higher than that line.

To adjust the stem, loosen the expansion bolt near the top. Don't remove it. When you're finished, retighten the bolt enough so that the bar doesn't shift, but not too tightly. Here's how to test proper tightness: Stand in front of the bike with the front wheel held between your knees. Twist hard on the handlebars. The stem should rotate, but only a little and after much effort.

Accessories

Mountain bikes have all kinds of add-ons. They vary in price and necessity, but here are the most common ones:

- *Water bottle*. Drinking water is a must during a ride. Remember that you're going to be biking up in the mountains, on dusty trails.

Mountain Biking: Techniques and Tricks

- *Tire tool and hex-head wrench*. Tools are also a must on every ride! You will need the tire tool to help pry your tire off the rim when you get a flat. The hex-head wrench will help tighten bolts and adjust the seat, handlebars, wheels, brakes, and most other bicycle parts. Many lightweight tool sets that fit in your pocket or seat bag (see below) are available.
- *Hand pump*. This is a smaller version of the upright bicycle pump, made to be carried using a side mount. Hand pumps will save you from walking your bike home after a flat.
- *Inner-tube patch kit*. A patch kit should be able to repair most tires to the point where you can at least get back home or to the shop.
- *Seat bag*. Seat bags attach in back of and beneath the saddle using Velcro straps and are handy for holding tools, money, ID cards, or snacks.

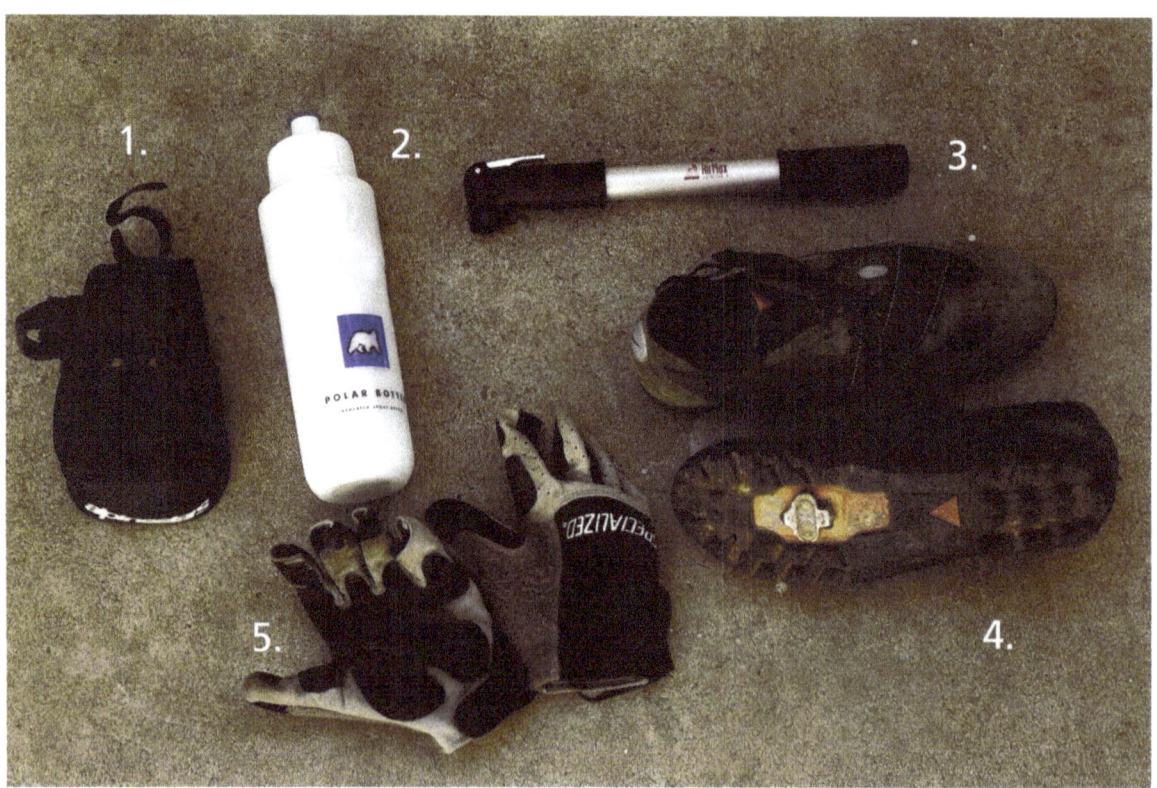

Some essential accessories to take with you off-road biking include:
1. seat bag **2.** water bottle **3.** hand pump **4.** mountain biking shoes
5. full-fingered gloves

The Right Bike for You

- *Bar ends*. Bar ends extend your handlebars by attaching to the ends at a right angle. Bar ends let you change hand positions so your arms and back don't get stiff, and help on steep climbs.
- *Clipless pedals*. Clipless pedals let you attach your shoes directly to the pedals. This allows you to pedal more easily and jump higher, because your feet are attached to the bike and you can pull it up with you. Most clipless pedals come standard with quality mountain bikes.
- *Shoes*. Bicycle shoes have hard soles and fit tightly to your feet. They also attach to clipless pedals to form a power unit with your legs.

Wearing a helmet and protective eyewear decreases the potential for injury. Make sure both fit securely.

Safety Gear

Accessories are always optional, but safety gear is a must. If you really have to, you can survive without bar ends or clipless pedals. That's not the case with a helmet.

Helmets

The single most important piece of gear, after the bike itself, is the helmet. Never ride without one. Some people claim helmets slow them down, but that just isn't true. Today's helmets are made of lightweight materials, so they really don't weigh bikers down. In fact, most helmets now are shaped to be aerodynamic and actually increase speed! There simply isn't any reason not to wear a helmet. The first time you take a serious fall, you'll be glad you had your helmet on.

Mountain Biking: Techniques and Tricks

Make sure the helmet you choose is comfortable. It should fit snugly but not too tightly. It should cover your forehead but not block your vision. You should buy a helmet that is certified by the American National Standards Institute (ANSI), the Snell Memorial Foundation, the Canadian Standards Association (CSA), or the American Society for Testing and Materials (ASTM).

Gloves

Wearing gloves helps your hands grip the handlebars. They also protect your hands in a fall. There are three types of gloves: full-finger, cut-off finger, and thermal (for winter rides). If you live in a northern climate and plan to ride during the winter, buy a pair of thermal gloves. Otherwise, lighter-weight gloves will be fine year-round. The difference between full-finger and cut-off finger styles is a matter of preference, though full-finger gloves offer the best overall protection.

Injuries

Mountain biking is fun, fast, and exciting—but it is also dangerous. Most bikers get injured at least once a year. Not surprisingly, the majority of the injuries happen while going down moderate or steep hills.

One of the keys to minimizing injury is knowing how to fall. The most important thing to do during a fall is to keep yourself loose. That way your body absorbs the impact more easily. Tightening up, sticking your legs or arms out, or fighting the fall can all cause more serious injuries.

During a fall, tuck yourself into a loose ball, head down, elbows in, and roll with the fall. Your butt and legs will take most of the shock instead of your elbows, knees, and head. Also, if you have time, try to kick away from your bike—you don't want it landing on you and possibly injuring you even more.

Once you've stopped moving, get up, dust yourself off, and check for cuts. If you're bleeding, press steadily on the cut with your hand until the bleeding stops. It's a good idea to carry some adhesive bandages and antibiotic ointment (Neosporin is one over-the-counter brand) in your seat bag. You can patch yourself up right away and be back on the trail in no time. For a more severe injury, ask for help from someone in your riding party or on the trail. If you feel dizzy at all, don't get back on your bike. Walk it out off the trail instead, and then go see a doctor immediately.

Practice

If you're not used to biking, you'll quickly discover that your whole body aches after a ride. It isn't just your legs that hurt after a hard ride. Your hands hurt from gripping the handlebars and working the brakes. Your arms and shoulders are tired from supporting your weight. Your back and stomach are tired from pedaling and taking the bumps. Your neck hurts from keeping your head and helmet up. Most mountain bikers claim that if you aren't hurting after a ride, you really haven't cycled.

The good news is that you'll get used to this pain, and your muscles will adapt. When you're starting out, just ride for a little while—an hour or so each day—to get used to the bike. After a few days of easy rides, increase the time to two hours. You want to be completely comfortable on the bike so that you can concentrate on the terrain on which you'll ride. Practice also gives you time to adjust the saddle, handlebars, and pedals to the right positions for your body.

Trail Wisdom

Rad sports athletes usually perform best when they take a lot of instruction and make it their own. Using each of these techniques will make you a better rider. Crafting your own way to ride using these techniques can make you a racing champion. Now it's time to ride!

Glossary

balance point The point where you either start dropping forward or back. This is the ideal place to hold and control a proper wheelie.

clipless The name for a pedal-and-shoe system where the clips or cleats clip onto the soles of special shoes. They're called "clipless" because you can't see the clips when you're clipped in.

endo A stationary front wheelie where the back wheel lifts off the ground and the front tire stays grounded. Also used to describe flying over the handlebars (an abbreviation of "end-over-end").

good foot The foot you automatically put forward when coasting.

line The desirable path or strategy to take on a tricky trail section.

spin A smooth pedal motion.

stand To maintain equilibrium during a certain period of time without pedaling or applying brake levers.

static A stopped position.

toe clips A clip-and-strap system that connects a rider's feet and toes to the pedals. Toe clips usually don't require special shoes.

wheelie Lifting the front wheel off the ground, usually with some combination of pulling on the handlebars, pedaling harder, and balance.

For More Information

Organizations

Adventure Cycling Association

150 East Pine Street
P.O. Box 8308
Missoula, MT 59807
(800) 755-2453
Web site: http://www.adv-cycling.org

Atlantic Canada Cycling

P.O. Box 1555, Station Central
Halifax, NS B3J 2Y3
Canada
(902) 423-2453
e-mail: cycling@atl-canadacycling.com
Web site: http://www.atl-canadacycling.com

Mountain Biking: Techniques and Tricks

International Mountain Biking Association (IMBA)

1121 Broadway, Suite 203
P.O. Box 7578
Boulder, CO 80306
(303) 545-9011
(888) 442-4622
Web site: http://www.imba.com

National Off-Road Bicycling Association (NORBA)

One Olympic Plaza
Colorado Springs, CO 80909
(719) 866-4581
Web Site: http://www.adventuresports.com

Women's Mountain Biking and Tea Society (WOMBATS)

P.O. Box 757
Fairfax, CA 94978
(415) 459-0980
Web site: http://www.wombats.org

Web Sites

Due to the changing nature of Internet links, the Rosen Publishing Group, Inc., has developed an online list of Web sites related to the subject of this book. This site is updated regularly. Please use this link to access the list:

http://www.rosenlinks.com/rs/mbtt/

For Further Reading

Amici Design. *Fat Tire: A Celebration of Mountain Biking*. San Francisco: Chronicle, 1999.

Crane, Nick, and Charles Kelly. *Richard's Mountain Bike Book*. New York: Ballantine, 1988.

Demattei, Susan, and Bill Strickland. *Mountain Biking: Over the Edge*. New York: McGraw-Hill, 1998.

Friel, Joe, and Ned Overend. *The Mountain Biker Training Bible: A Complete Training Guide for the Competitive Mountain Biker*. Boulder, CO: Velo Press, 2000.

Howard, John. *Dirt!: The Philosophy, Technique, and Practice of Mountain Biking*. New York: Lyons, 1997.

Hurd, Jim, and Jay Pridmore. *The American Bicycle*. New York: Motorbooks International, 2001.

Jones, Steve. *Mountain Bike Techniques*. Birmingham, AL: Menasha Ridge, 2001.

Lovett, Rick. *The Essential Touring Cyclist*. Chicago: McGraw-Hill, 2000.

Pavelka, Ed, ed. *Bicycling Magazine's Mountain Biking Skills: Tactics, Tip, and Techniques to Master Any Terrain*. Emmaus, PA: Rodale Press, 2000.

Zinn, Leonard. *Zinn and the Art of Mountain Bike Maintenance*, third edition. Chicago: Velo Press, 2000.

Bibliography

Anstiss, Brendan. "Mountain Bike Injuries." New Zealand Mountain Bike Web. Retrieved January 10, 2002 (http://www.mountainbike.co.nz/politics/articles/anstiss/chapter2.html).

DIY. "Introduction to Mountain Biking." Retrieved January 10, 2002 (http://www.diynet.com/DIY/article/0,2058,5646,FF.html).

McCain, Matthew. "Mountain Biking." Retrieved January 10, 2002 (http://www.cob.montevallo.edu/student/McCainMJ/default.htm).

The Mountain Bike Hall of Fame. Retrieved January 10, 2002 (http://www.mtnbikehalloffame.com/home.cfm).

"Mountain Biking." Retrieved January 10, 2002 (http://library.thinkquest.org/11569/html_home/html_mbiking/mbiking.html).

Schloss, David. "Bike Helmets: Keeping It Covered." GORP.com. Retrieved January 10, 2002 (http://www.gorp.com/gorp/gear/biking/helmets.htm).

ScottishSport.co.uk. "Cycle Disciplines." Retrieved January 10, 2002 (http://www.scottishsport.co.uk/cycling/disciplines.htm).

Strassman, Mike. "Mountain Bike Maintenance." GORP.com. Retrieved January 10, 2002 (http://www.gorp.com/gorp/publishers/ics/bik_main.htm).

"The Sport of Bicycling." Retrieved January 10, 2002 (http://library.thinkquest.org/11569/html_home/).

Index

A

accessories, 37–39

B

bicycles, history of, 7–10
braking/brakes, 12–13, 34
Breeze, Joe, 7, 10
bunny hop, 29–30

C

climbing hills, 17–21
cornering, 23–24
cross-country competitions, 11
cyclocross bikes, 7

D

derailleur gears, 6–7, 9, 14
descending, 21–23
downhill competitions, 11
downhill switchback, 25
drop-off, the, 31–32

F

Fisher, Gary, 7, 9, 10

G

gears, shifting, 14
gear shifters, types of, 14

H

handlebars, adjusting, 37, 41
hop, the, 30–31

I

injuries, 40–41

K

Kelly, Charles, 7, 10
"klunkers," 7

M

mountain bikes
    adjusting, 34–37
    buying, 33–34
    hybrids, 33
mountain biking
    beginning skills, 12–16
    biking conduct, 8–9
    buying a bike, 33–34

Mountain Biking: Techniques and Tricks

competitions, 11
history of, 6–7, 9–10
practicing, 41
trail techniques and tricks, 17–32
training, 11

N

National Off-Road Bicycle Association (NORBA), 11

O

obstacles, getting over, 26–32

P

pedal kick, 23, 26, 28, 31
pedals, adjusting, 35, 41

R

Ritchey, Tom, 7, 10

S

saddle/seat, adjusting, 35–37, 38, 41
safety gear, 39–40
Scott, John Finley, 6–7
spinning, 16

T

trackstand, 15

W

wheelie, 31, 32
Woodsie Bike, 6–7

About the Author

Aaron Rosenberg was born in New Jersey, grew up in New Orleans, and now lives in New York. He has taught college English, has worked in corporate graphics, and now runs his own game publishing company, Clockworks. He has written short stories, essays, poems, articles, novels, books, and role-playing games.

Acknowledgements

Thanks to Kathy Sessler and Harry Leary

Credits

Cover, pp. 10, 13–16, 18–32, 35, 36, 38, 39 © Tony Donaldson/Icon SMI/Rosen Publishing.; pp. 4–5 © Richard Radstone//Corbis; p. 7 © Hulton-Deutsch Collection/Corbis;

Design and Layout

Les Kanturek